LIGATURES

LIGATURES

By

JAMES FERRIS

Selections from Books I - VI were published as *Mastications* in June 2008. Selections from Book VII appeared in *Gandt 3* in October 2008.

Ferris, James, 1980 -
Ligatures / James Ferris
p. cm.
ISBN 978-1-906496-35-7
1. Aphorisms—Apothegms—Miscellanea 2. Ties—Neckwear 3. Diaries—Memoirs

Typeset in 10.5pt Sabon

Contents

Preface

This year began under the auspices of a single constraint, that I would wear a different tie each day. Simple as the task may appear, this sartorial experiment has held considerable sway over my life; as the uroboric loop of a year wraps itself around me, I draw together my reflections and present you with as vivid a self-portrait as I can muster. The book consists of twelve sections, tiered by days, and chronological in fashion. I hereby tie the final knot.

J.F.

London, December 31, 2008

i

"The name of the bow is life; its work is death."
— Heraclitus

LIGATURES

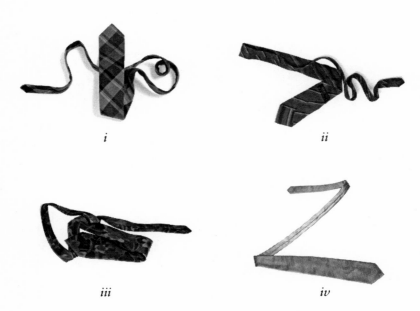

i

ii

iii

iv

1

BOOK I

1

A starting point will often be a full stop.

2

Large ladies know how little men feel.

3

Shaking out the optimism of the pan glosses over the pessimism of the brush.

4

A questioning nature will even roll its tongue into the shape of a question mark when reaching for a pea.

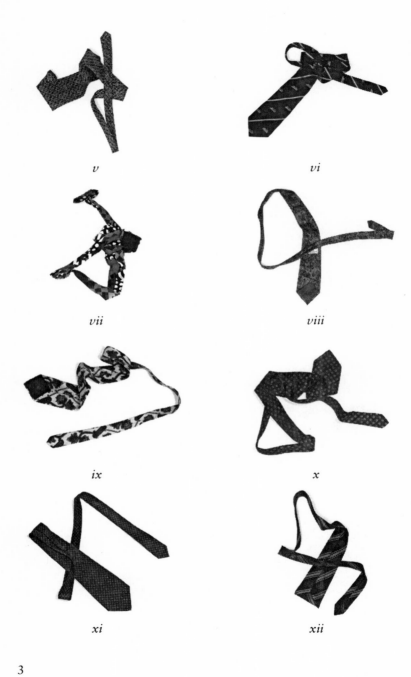

v   *vi*

vii   *viii*

ix   *x*

xi   *xii*

BOOK I

5

Dressing up and dumbing down.

6

Ruled by one; mauled by many.

7

A diary will wake with a bad neck if a window has been kept open all night.

8

Ears wounded by suggestion.

9

Pars pro toto.— Not understanding why someone is walking in a certain manner we must try on their shoes, but first we must try on their trousers.

10

If it feels right, feel again.

11

Titles often try to tell you that there is a head attached to the body.

12

If you do something for long enough, the people who initially found you very annoying will applaud you, and the people who applauded you initially will find you very annoying.

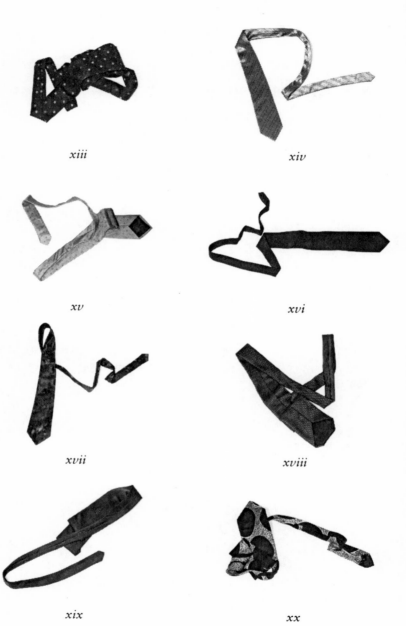

xiii

xiv

xv

xvi

xvii

xviii

xix

xx

5

BOOK I

13

Divine beauty: bovine duty.

14

Collaboration: one does the work whilst the other keeps their cool.

15

Thoughts out of season are too often served with a garnish.

16

Be stern, act swift, lest the rabble lay you down.

17

The greatest affront to his life was that his books were never banned.

18

His great talent lay in producing works of art that left enough room for the viewer to imagine what it would have been like if they had been produced by someone of great talent.

19

Grassy roots make for brassy boots.

20

Exercise, like style, consists in studied and exaggerated repetition: the former is designed to take your breath away, the latter that of others.

xxi

xxii

xxiii

xxiv

xxv

xxvi

xxvii

xxviii

BOOK I

21

When I wear my words short and tight, my tongue is like a stick of dynamite.

22

Losing voice: losing home.

23

Just because she glows in the dark doesn't mean she will glow in the light.

24

Thugs in love; kissing with fists.

25

A scantily clad sentence will hold your attention by revealing some of its intention in a teasing manner.

26

Nature is never naked.

27

The complete fragments . . . . how incomplete this sentence seems.

28

Raw meat has the audacity to unnerve, to remind us that we are never quite ourselves; but flesh gorging in excess of pleasure, enjoyed to the size of a life.

xxix

xxx

xxxi

BOOK I

29

Ideas sit lightly on the posterior of sleep.

30

Ironed in youth and creased by age.

31

A good tailor would improve his manners no end.

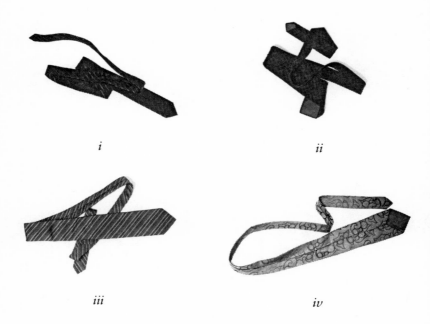

i

ii

iii

iv

BOOK II

1

Perfecting a practice is the surest way to lose any pleasure in practising.

2

Art can also wear too much foundation.

3

When paraphrasing, you may as well mangle the author's name too. – Majes Rifers

4

Imagination often runs away with the footnotes.

v

vi

vii

viii

vix

x

xi

xii

BOOK II

5

Safety is the greatest danger to sense.

6

The lash of the wit stings those it licks.

7

His disdain for life only washed out when he kicked the bucket.

8

The thumb says less than the finger.

9

She wrote just like an untuned radio.

10

Catching up on sleep as with an old friend whose company we never tire of.

11

The thinnest of words have the fattest of meanings.

12

There should be a jab to remedy the malaise caused by the sound bite.

13

A great wit weights grit to throw the right amount.

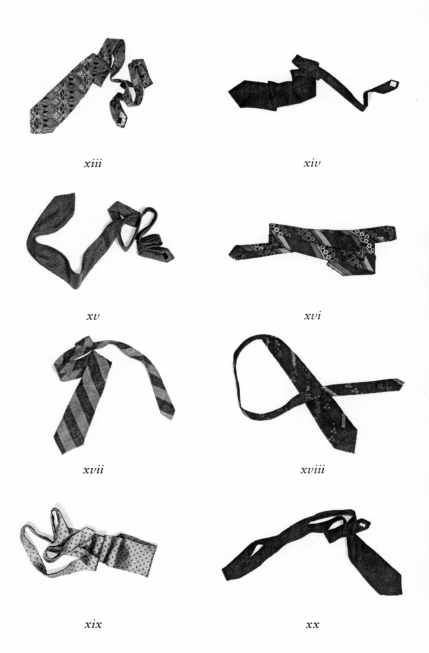

xiii

xiv

xv

xvi

xvii

xviii

xix

xx

BOOK II

14

Only once before have I come across a book that could scream quite like that.

15

Time must have passed slowly before it had time to grind the pebbles to sand.

16

I can never keep the tempo of a thought without enough room to pace.

17

Learning and yearning are two steps from earning.

18

I always check the last date stamped in a book that I want to borrow: if the date is within the last five years, I politely decline its company and continue to look for one that has slept long enough not to sound tired.

19

Always judge a book by its cover of dust.

20

This is a health club madam, 'health' being the operative word.

21

Art imitates nurture.

xxi

xxii

xxiii

xxiv

xxv

xxvi

xxvii

xxviii

BOOK II

22

His face contorted in anger as if it were being sucked into the black hole vacated by the brain.

23

Lack of taste is the sign of a highly developed palate.

24

Reason is tantamount to treason when it thinks itself more important than the ruling body.

25

Sharing interests is fine, but make sure that you gain on their account.

26

Work made imagining an audience imagines an audience wrongly if it imagines it with any imagination.

27

Eyes are never sorry glancing when excused by the spectacle of dancing.

28

An artist with a problem is like a cat with a ball of string: the artist feels surprise at every unexpected movement as if the ball were really alive; each gesture creates a new knot that looks increasingly impossible to trace back to the tidy impression of the ball, just as each knot would be simple to untie if the artist were not tied up in there too.

xxix

BOOK II

29

Etna – the finest mountain escape.

i

ii

iii

iv

BOOK III

1

I can't help myself; all I can do is help myself.

2

Too many authors are like limescale encrusting the filament of their ideas.

3

What is needed is a pair of scissors that cuts both ways.

4

On the tip of the tongue it delights; at the back of the throat it chokes.

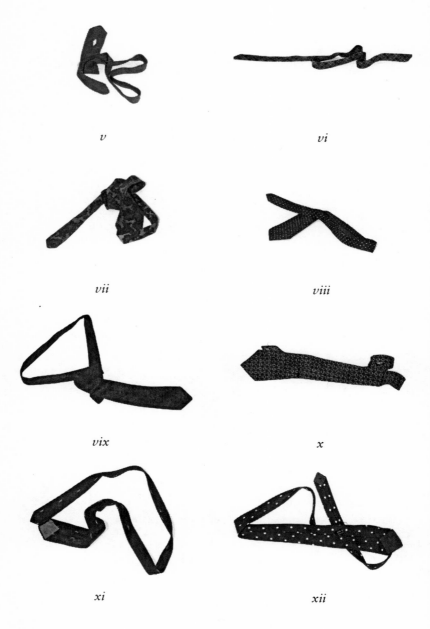

v

vi

vii

viii

vix

x

xi

xii

BOOK III

5

Each humour lacking inches immobile.

6

Nerves express you like a brush stroke.

7

Overhearing a conversation in which the couple conversing were also overhearing their own conversation: "Bailey's bottom was dripping with saliva when he left there."

8

Books flower as they drown.

9

To read into a tie the ills of humanity; and as for the knot. . .

10

The attempts to fit great works of literature into nutshells requires a very refined reader with a very fine pair of nutcrackers.

11

A perfectly serious survey could be carried out about artists who look like their work; self-portraits would be found to bear the least likeness.

12

When looking for the new, be thankful that there is no key to obstruct your view.

xiii

xiv

xv

xvi

xvii

xviii

xix

xx

BOOK III

13

Time is in the habit of pulling faces.

14

Arrogance is seated on the shoulders.

15

Who can but help follow their nose?

16

Only fingers that know how to dance will wonder.

17

Fool hardy in laurel leaves.

18

Better to be perspired against than to be conspired against.

19

Reading an introduction often feels like being offered someone's leftovers in a restaurant.

20

The metre rules our lives just as the yard once hemmed in our livestock.

21

His laughter was the funniest thing about him.

xxi

xxii

xxiii

xxiv

xxv

xxvi

xxvii

xxviii

BOOK III

22

I often get bored in my sleep and fast-forward through a conversation that I think I already know the outcome of; in my agitation I skip myself out of the dream altogether.

23

Borrow an idea and use it by all means, but for goodness sake give it back when you have finished with it.

24

Having spent the night with Proust, the morning could be nothing but mannered.

25

Pivoting on the knot of a full stop.— Death feels the final shape of life.

26

The muscle of difficulty; a natural sunshade.

27

Without the right technique, mopping a floor can make it look dirtier than it was before. As with art: although it may smell fresh, it has merely mashed together all the things that it wanted to wipe away.

28

The danger with subtlety is that it easily gets mistaken for something it is not. The danger with irony is that it easily gets mistaken for something that it is.

xxix

xxx

xxxi

BOOK III

29

Travelling from A to A, separated by the pangram of a day.

30

An eviction order served by the OED.

31

Words start from scratch and end being kicked by habit.

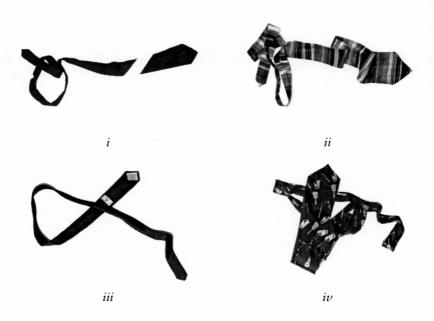

i

ii

iii

iv

BOOK IV

1

One-liners make it hard to read between the lines.

2

Imagine the most literal demonstration of the most abstract concept.

3

Getting a tie to match a shirt is as difficult as getting a work of art to fit a context.

4

Novelty ties: exclamation marks standing on their heads.

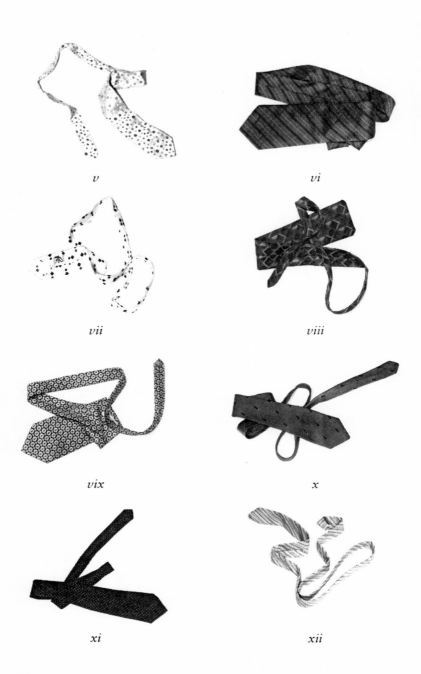

v

vi

vii

viii

vix

x

xi

xii

BOOK IV

5

It's not what you eat; it's the way that you eat it.

6

Enough is a meagre bout of too much.

7

Research in art: artistic vision has now been replaced by artistic revision.

8

The next big thing: stilts walking on stilts.

9

The sign of the times should tell you in which direction not to go.

10

The sun and the mirror burn holes through people's lives.

11

You may have to search all day to find a chestnut that isn't old.

12

The infamous and the unfamous are on first name terms.

13

Be thankful that most days pass without a punch line.

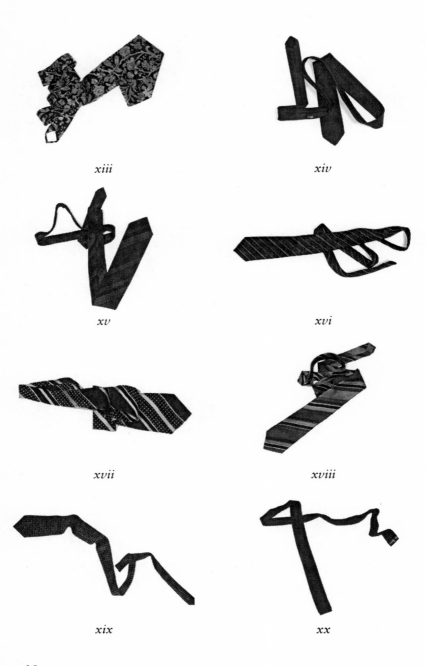

xiii

xiv

xv

xvi

xvii

xviii

xix

xx

35

BOOK IV

14

It is impossible to see ourselves as others do because we are always standing in the way.

15

The quickest way to lose attachment with a friend is to rip them off.

16

Every breath is a sigh of relief when it is not a scream.

17

Growing immature with unadulterated age.

18

Take advantage of your distractions and you will get a lot undone.

19

The dissatisfaction of feet hurrying to escape each place they step, until they reach the place where they need step no more.

20

Pure filth: at least you admit that it has quality; even dirt has a degree.

21

Knee-jerk reactions. — The worst kind of sinner runs on their knees to confess.

xxi

xxii

xxiii

xxiv

xxv

xxvi

xxvii

xxviii

BOOK IV

22

Anorexia is all-consuming: Obesity is consuming all.

23

A sweater whose label exclaimed "forever relaxin'" looked stretched, as if the fibres themselves had become lazy and were slouching along with the words, spoken by a mouth stuffed with food.

24

Looking great: the sensation of slicing a narrow path through the world.

25

In a library where there is nowhere to hide, thinking has no folly, and blushed skin shows how quickly a gaze can empty a head.

26

A windowless house is a grave affair.

27

Speaking to animals is a public display: I heard a man shout at his dog: "You know the rules!"; what he was really shouting was: "I am a man of rules."

28

How many times have we shrugged off a beautiful work of art as soon as we have found out that somebody beautiful has made it?

xxix   *xxx*

BOOK IV

29

Kissing stops the tongue from lashing out of bounds.

30

Pulling a Duchenne smile.

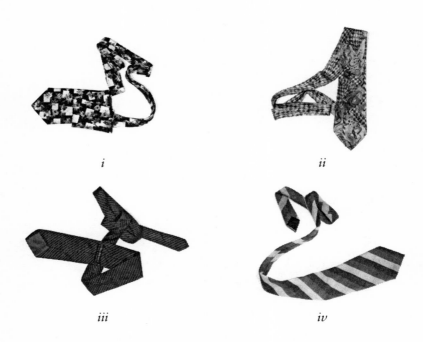

i

ii

iii

iv

BOOK V

1

Stones have years where they don't have ears.

2

Many mistakes are grossly exaggerated by being buried too close to the surface.

3

Read all about it.
(Errata: for Read read Read)

4

Revolting sentences.— Bullying words into a sentence will condemn them to hard labour.

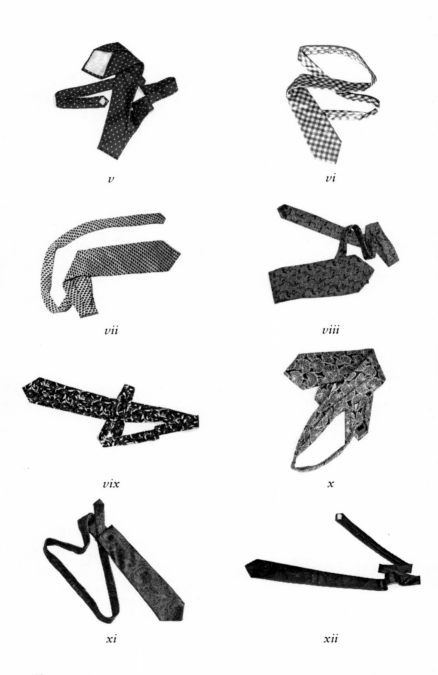

v

vi

vii

viii

vix

x

xi

xii

BOOK V

5

We become whom we are by being seen at a distance and recognised as someone else.

6

Find an analogy, use the analogy; forget that it's an analogy.

7

Fashion tip: wear pink in the sun to get that chameleon look.

8

The book was bound to keep silent, with the odds numbering the same as the evens.

9

Not being sure of the meaning suggests that in fact it wasn't well meant.

10

We give a slight impression of ourselves when we outline our past purely by the light of our successes.

11

It is often more reassuring to receive no compliment at all.

12

The problem with subtlety is that four out of five will find it too subtle and seven out of ten will find it too obvious; the others were taking no notice.

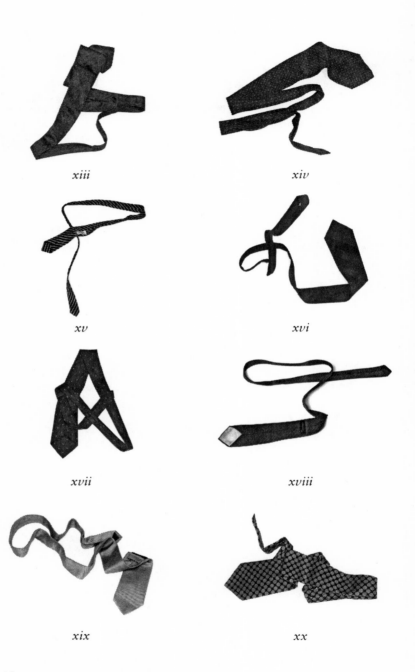

xiii

xiv

xv

xvi

xvii

xviii

xix

xx

13

Newly refurbished.— Too many miles are wasted deciding in which direction not to go.

14

Everything for sale bar quality.

15

Opinions, like flags, should be tested in strong weather to see if they retain their shape. Some flags look deceptively like others when draped in a certain manner and some look absurd when flown at full mast. The best flags do not associate with an ideal but are themselves that ideal.

16

Repeat a word until it becomes absurd.

17

Fame for the French is a hunger.

18

When a statement rings too easily true it most likely has a better half.

19

Time, in its turn, has me to spare.

20

The sharpest point will also be blunt.

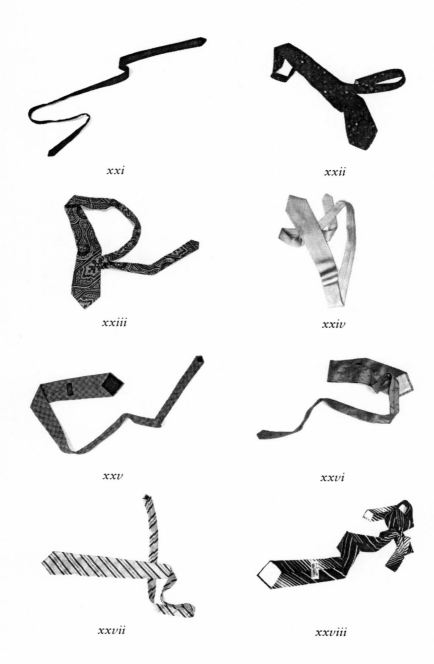

xxi

xxii

xxiii

xxiv

xxv

xxvi

xxvii

xxviii

47

BOOK V

21

It appeared that the thesaurus was all that he had read.

22

A tip added automatically to the bill leads you to the conclusion that what you just ate was *just* nice.

23

The by-product of her art was that she became a product.

24

Someone who claims that they can't dance will often dance as adequately as someone who claims that they can, if you ask them to show you what they *don't* mean by dancing.

25

Timing is more important than the notes played; punctuation can make or break a career.

26

The only art I find socially acceptable is anti-social through and through.

27

Her texting etiquette leaves a lot to be desired.

28

It is not surprising that Flaubert found them so stupid: he had read all of the books for them.

xxix

xxx

xxxi

BOOK V

29

We chew papers when we're young, and later they chew us.

30

Wolves howling, bitten by lunar ticks.

31

The distance from A to B is always twenty-four steps.

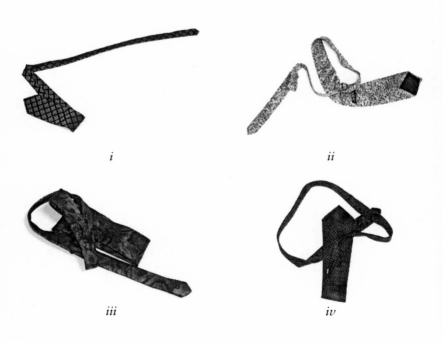

i

ii

iii

iv

51

BOOK VI

1

Plain is seldom simple; nice is never easy.

2

You have said it enough that it has become trite true.

3

Being original used to mean being the first; now it means being the second and the third.

4

A string of associations will tie you in knots if you try to find the beginning or the end.

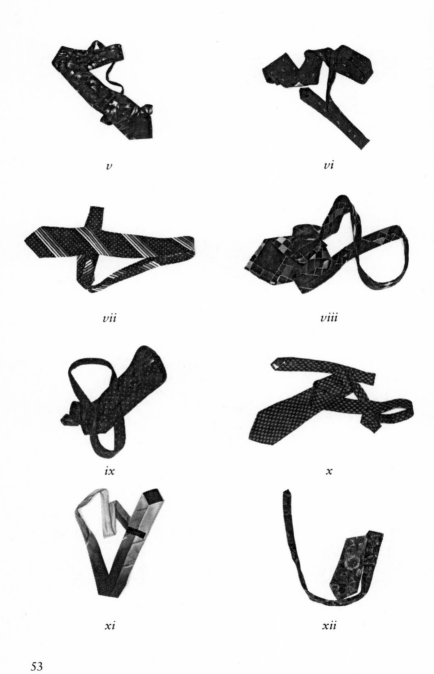

v

vi

vii

viii

ix

x

xi

xii

5

Eccentric to the core.

6

Some artists become so concerned with making it that they are no longer concerned with what it is they are making. Once they have made it they must make it again and again; they become the maid of their own making.

7

Don't knock it before you've entered.

8

A pun can drain as much as it can clog.

9

Shop till you drop, buy till you die.

10

The fattest of words have the thinnest of meanings.

11

Little did he know that the little that he knew meant a lot to the few who knew that little bit about him.

12

The fame of Wittgenstein lies in the fact that almost everybody knows the first *and* the last line of his book. If that is the case then the rest we must pass over in silence.

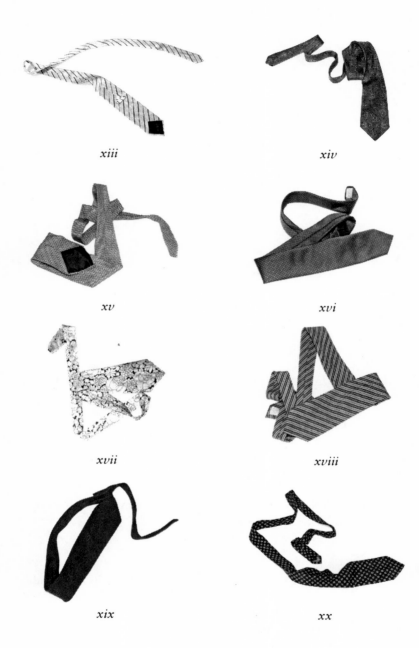

xiii

xiv

xv

xvi

xvii

xviii

xix

xx

BOOK VI

13

The chair sat on the floor, the man sat on the chair, the hair sat on the man, the hat sat on the hair and the air sat on the hat.

14

Always judge a painting by its cover.

15

Adequate analogies make that which is being analogised seem inadequate.

16

When everything is seen as a fragment, something significant can be read into the smallest insignificance. . .

17

. . . banana slippers.

18

I was once asked as a boy what flagellation meant. I replied: "It has something to do with the heart", and how right I was.

19

At a certain goldsmiths they have made the groundbreaking discovery of how to reverse the alchemical process.

20

An artist should hold off their pride, to wait and see what springs from their child.

xxi

xxii

xxiii

xxiv

xxv

xxvi

xxvii

xxviii

BOOK VI

21

Not until I start to write do I start to read.

22

An aphorism must be judged on how tender it is to bite into and how viciously it bites back.

23

An eye infection takes the pleasure out of seeing and the pleasure out of not seeing.

24

Legend has it that he couldn't even read his own legend.

25

His pockets filled with glee when in a handshake he detected an easy sale.

26

Retort in their native tongue and watch their grin go.

27

Abysmal curiosity will find things hard to fathom if it seeks beyond the surface.

28

What goes down must come up.— Nothing is more off-putting than seeing your words coming out of another persons mouth exactly as they went in.

xxix   *xxx*

BOOK VI

29

My passport forgot me.

30

A half-wit is rarely even that.

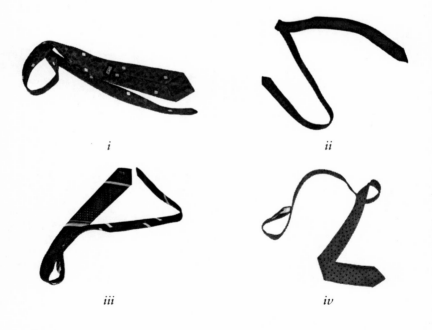

i

ii

iii

iv

BOOK VII

1

Interpretation can make the world seem upside down if the wings
are flapping harder at the feet than at the head.

2

A perforated book of punch lines.

3

Quite often the very fact of owning a book will make the idea of
reading it seem preposterous: to this I owe my entire library.

4

Fitness first: fatness seconds.

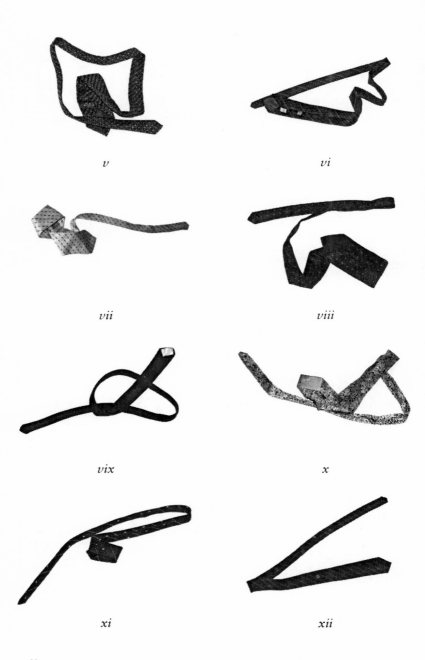

v

vi

vii

viii

vix

x

xi

xii

BOOK VII

5

In the throes of an illness I had the sense that my skin was as delicate as candyfloss, but that if I tasted it then it would have the bitterness of bile.

6

It is difficult to listen to music when all you can hear is the hair-cut.

7

Site specificity sights its specificity in order to blind the viewer to its limitations. It is like someone showing off their extraordinary deformity with pride and self-pity at the same time.

8

There is no real reason to believe that the real reason behind an action is more reasonable to believe than the reason that you would like others to believe is real.

9

Accessibility to a work of art is like an exit sign illuminated in a theatre – fearing for our safety we forget about the play.

10

On a jogging machine.— We feel that we are getting somewhere only when we are going nowhere.

11

When he turned the water into wine he also coined the phrase 'drunk as a fish'.

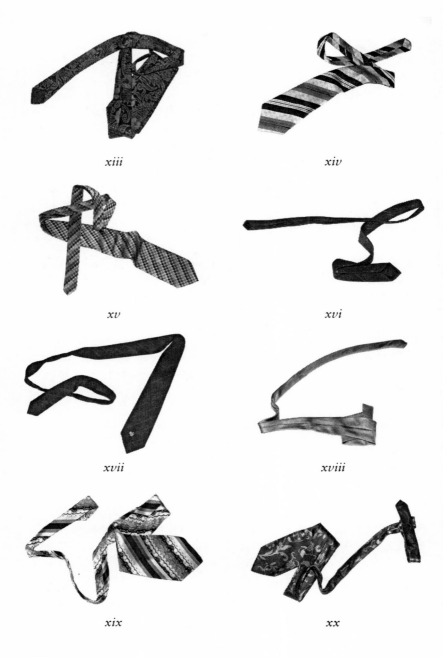

xiii

xiv

xv

xvi

xvii

xviii

xix

xx

BOOK VII

12

Mirrors betray as much as they obey.

13

The flea that jumped into my eye, drowned in the tear that it made me cry.

14

It is not the size that counts but the shape.

15

Plunder and blunder are so close that they hold hands wherever they go.

16

Desire to eat a city; washing ones mouth out with bricks and mortar.

17

The new tastes of a new place; fresh buildings. Hot eyes dart as if they were excited molecules, dancing molten on an unknown street.

18

The greatest bores carry the heaviest burden; the heaviest thing to heave is a sigh.

19

The evidence keeps building that the Romans were obsessed with celery.

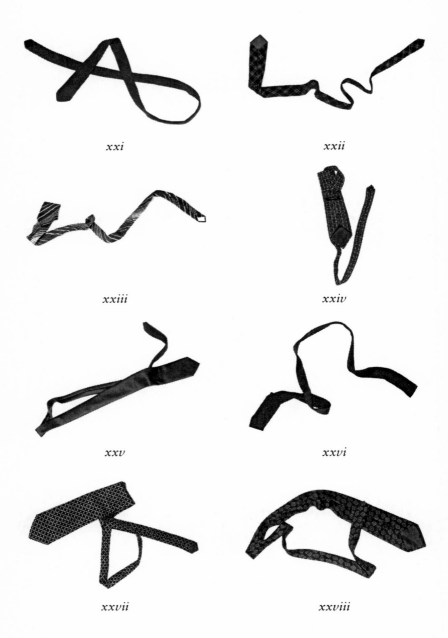

xxi

xxii

xxiii

xxiv

xxv

xxvi

xxvii

xxviii

BOOK VII

20

Charm attacks.

21

Expats make a bad smell wherever they land.

22

Boredom buries us like a landslide.

23

The truth is not set like a table.

24

The cross roads raged.

25

Rarity is overcooked when it is not treated simply as a matter of taste.

26

The question should perhaps be: "How old have you been?"

27

Explaining things in layman's terms must still be sung in tune.

28

Give everyone their say, but please, tell them what to say in advance.

xxix

xxx

xxxi

BOOK VII

29

He had the face of an oboe but the laughter of a piccolo.

30

In the case of Tolstoy, it was the Count that thought.

31

He who holds the handle handles the hole.

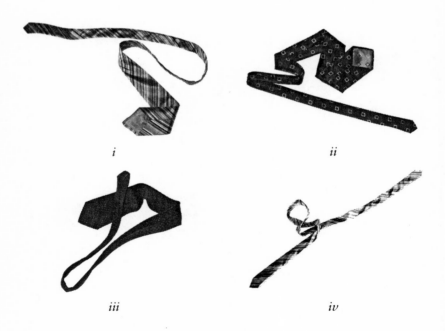

i

ii

iii

iv

BOOK VIII

1

Even socks do not comfort odd feet.

2

Imitation is the greatest mistake that innovates.

3

You wouldn't have thought the half-arsed would find it so comfortable to sit around for so long.

4

New notebooks are filled in advance with the tedium of knowing that there will be no new breakthrough.

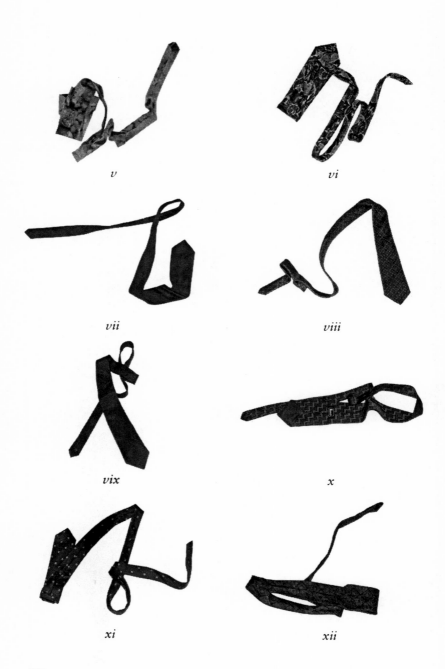

v

vi

vii

viii

vix

x

xi

xii

BOOK VIII

5

I punched a rose; a rose punctured I.

6

Looked at and loved at.

7

Private confession: public obsession.

8

Remember that celebrity was once a dirty word.

9

The eyesore truly was a sight for sore eyes.

10

Make up won't make believe.

11

The love greedy want amore and more.

12

We find the same great things pleasing: this displeases me greatly.

13

Doing justice to an idea doesn't always entail the most expensive lawyer.

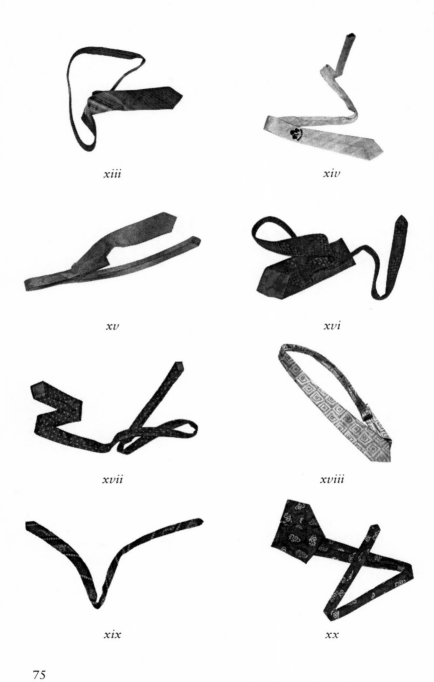

xiii

xiv

xv

xvi

xvii

xviii

xix

xx

BOOK VIII

14

What amazing good fortune to have chosen the right opinion.

15

Every day is a year away.

16

Hungry words gurn.

17

One needs to be consumed by someone else not to have enough of oneself.

18

Chance is a symptom, not a cure.

19

Ideas are sometimes as hard to pull off as ears.

20

What I would give for someone with an ounce of lightness.

21

We are always waiting but never know what for. How big does a miracle have to be?

22

I before he except after she.

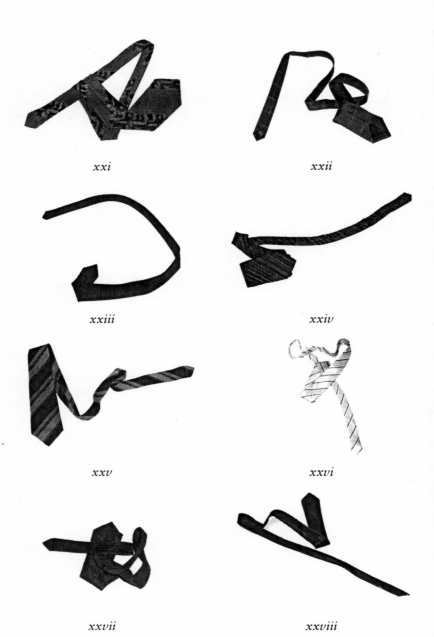

xxi

xxii

xxiii

xxiv

xxv

xxvi

xxvii

xxviii

BOOK VIII

23

I want simplicity, like a snail slowly advancing toward a barking dog, deaf to the situation.

24

Hearing a creek in the floorboards and being struck dumb by the thought: now I have to be fake again.

25

Catch yourself saying hello and notice how many different ways you say it, what parts of your face you use, where your eyes are cast; where your meaning is placed. A 'hello' can be strewn on stony ground or presented as an antique charm; a valuable relic from a formal time now departed.

26

'Entertainment' has the same ring to it as 'exit wound'.

27

The common share a great deal.

28

Dream about a fierce river: at points the water, flowing from one bank to the other, folded back on itself and formed a perfectly cylindrical vortex. I was on a raft with several others, constantly being swept off, only to struggle back on again. A horse was battling the tide next to the raft and kept trying to tell me where he was from; all I could make out was 'Near York'. I eventually ascertained that he was a close friend of my cousin in New York. I woke up disconcerted: I do not have a cousin in New York.

xxix

xxx

xxxi

BOOK VIII

29

Why is authenticity always so bad at using a hammer?

30

Simplicity expects nothing but sincerity.

31

Unsubtle souls unsettle themselves.

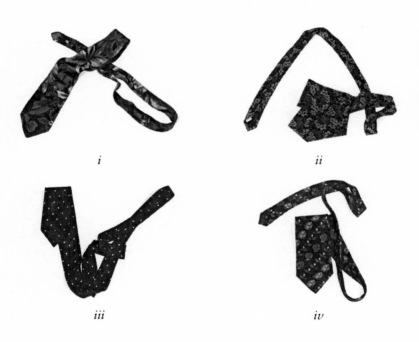

i

ii

iii

iv

BOOK IX

1

Some mouths continually fill with full stops.

2

Sentences can also be rare, medium or well done.

3

The difference between saying "I didn't mean it" and "the words didn't mean it".

4

Only in such a godforsaken place could there be so many believers.

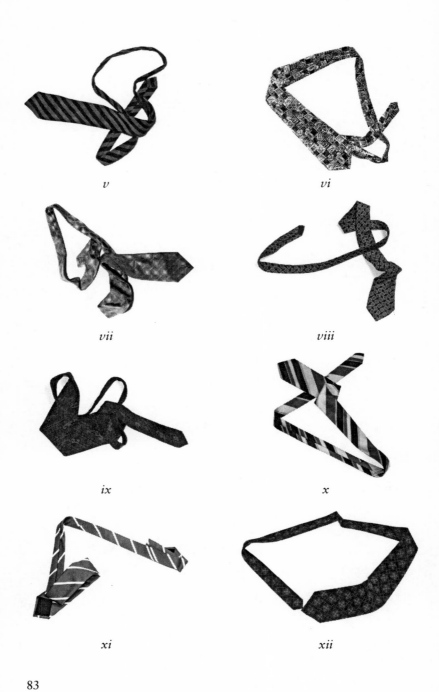

v

vi

vii

viii

ix

x

xi

xii

BOOK IX

5

You can write the word dog and it doesn't have to look like a dog, but some people think it should bark.

6

A story about a man who never forgot an insult; who never forgave a thing.

7

Jumping to a conclusion will verily scare it away.

8

The class of failure in art should not be 'failed' but 'untitled'.

9

I can envisage a lottery in which the possibility of random excessive gain is equally balanced by that of mindless and catastrophic ruin.

10

Rivers and roads have no fixed abodes.

11

When trade marks a word its lifeline is cut.

12

Many maxims are like daily horoscope forecasts: due to their teasing ambiguity there appears to be a hidden meaning, and through trying it on for size we stretch it to fit our lives.

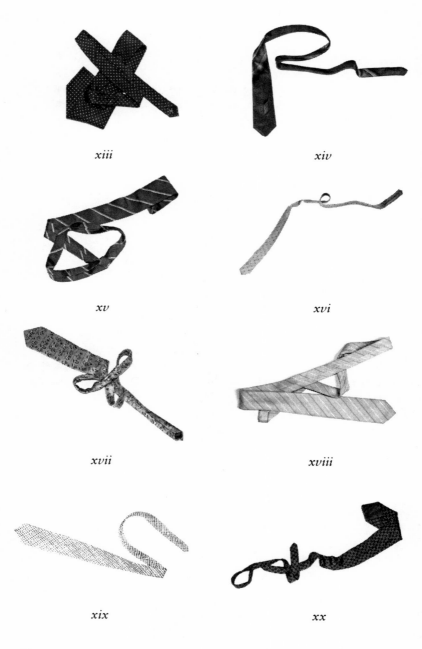

xiii

xiv

xv

xvi

xvii

xviii

xix

xx

BOOK IX

13

He had the unfortunate habit of seeing footnotes wherever he strode.

14

By adding a simple hat, a rule can form a role.

15

Semi-skimmed misreadings.

16

Forced meat of a maxim: a sausage of a saying.

17

The era can never shut out the sound of its own screaming.

18

The most wonderful bodies do the vilest of things, whilst the vilest of bodies do the most wonderful things.

19

Children's books are printed in large print, not in relation to their visual abilities, as large print is for the elderly, but in relation to the tempo of their reading: many books would benefit from such an imposed slowness.

20

Lacking the ability to keep silent, he even tells you he has nothing to say.

xxi

xxii

xxiii

xxiv

xxv

xxvi

xxvii

xxviii

BOOK IX

21

Flattery deflates piety into pomp.

22

"You've got some knees there haven't you girl?" I overheard an old man stating quite factually to a tourist.

23

A book of aphorisms is like an all-you-can-eat buffet: if you try everything at once you will fail to taste a thing.

24

The pun that invented the glue stick; how many inventions must have emerged from wordplay alone?

25

Perhaps an ambition would be to end with the words: I have suffered a beautiful life.

26

He knew his nous so well it almost strangled him.

27

Each zero fantasizes about having a number below him to sit upon.

28

Life, stretching from birth, will reach its limit and snap back beyond its point of departure.

xxix   *xxx*

BOOK IX

29

Whistling wears the lips like slippers.

30

Where are my trouser notes?

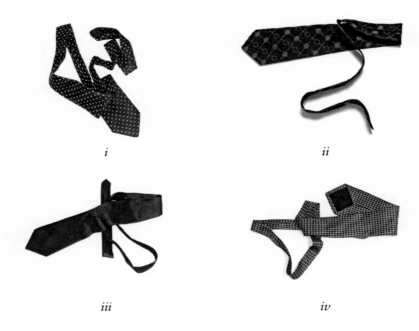

i

ii

iii

iv

BOOK X

1

The Holy Ghost: A Ghostly Hole.

2

Overhearing forces the imagination to swell, just as overeating does the stomach.

3

Finished projects close their eyes to the future; completion is an indiscretion that I would rather avoid.

4

Loeb Classics require a Latin left ear to be read.

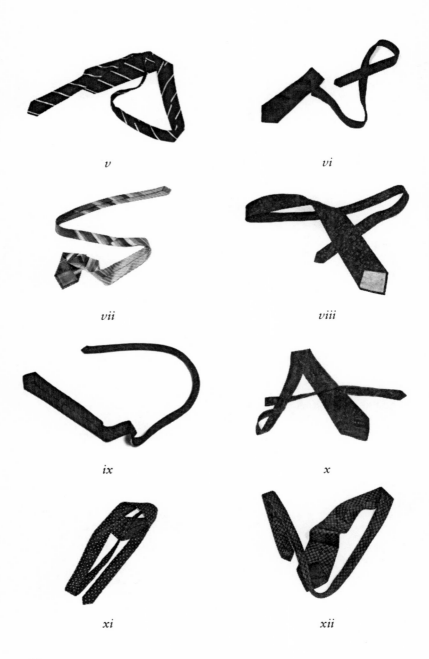

v

vi

vii

viii

ix

x

xi

xii

BOOK X

5

Art is the great disappearing act.

6

Endless pith: if I found a pip I wouldn't know what to do with it.

7

Life without a forwarding address.

8

Always judge a song by its cover.

9

Glancing across a tome is enough to turn your eyes to stone.

10

Love is consumed in the process of making it.

11

A town inhabited entirely by artists would be like a tool box filled entirely by spanners.

12

Problems come and grow.

13

A sentence is the duration upon which meaning hangs.

xiii

xiv

xv

xvi

xvii

xviii

xix

xx

BOOK X

14

Harmony is set like a broken arm.

15

"Daddy, put your children in the bin." I overheard a child demanding of her father.

16

Wise teeth rarely cheat; wisdom teeth rarely chatter.

17

Delirium cries out from the limbs, whilst melodrama clings to the face.

18

Cross disciplines try to tighten their loose trousers with the buckle of an 'and'.

19

Man is the whole who covers the sewer of life with shame.

20

Two types of artist: those who work from the neck up and those who work from the neck down; though a third type has been known: those who are nothing but neck.

21

Imitate to the best of your abilities, but don't forget that your abilities, at best, are imitations too.

xxi

xxii

xxiii

xxiv

xxv

xxvi

xxvii

xxviii

22

The pen that doesn't seep, sleeps.

23

Pneumonoultramicroscopicsilicovolcanokoniosis: may cause breathlessness or irritability.

24

Three years under an asbestos roof and my increased daily fibre intake hasn't had the health benefits I had hoped for.

25

Scented words carried on foul breath; foul words on sweet breath: one we pay for, the other we pray for.

26

Is there something deceptive about the term 'natural dye'?

27

A fit mind and a thoughtful body: my body is thoughtful when it makes the right moves, my mind is fit when it reaches the right conclusions. But what does the 'right' mean here? Right for a specific purpose?

28

Stumbling upon an attractive idea and thinking that it's too good to be true, meaning in fact that it's too true to be good: when a truth presents itself naked and perfectly formed in front of us, we must question whether we are the first.

xxix

xxx

xxxi

BOOK X

29

Technology takes root when its time is up.

30

In every flame a myth is read.

31

The trees wag their tails, excited by the wind's return.

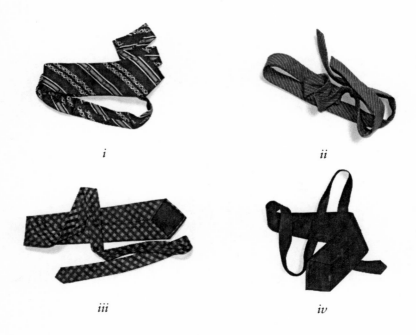

i

ii

iii

iv

BOOK XI

1

Crowds en masse sweat with an air of religiosity.

2

The present is future proof.

3

Shakespeare had the soul of an angel and the mind of a hundred monkeys.

4

Public Schooling.— Artists who make their mistakes in public find that soon all the public wants are their mistakes.

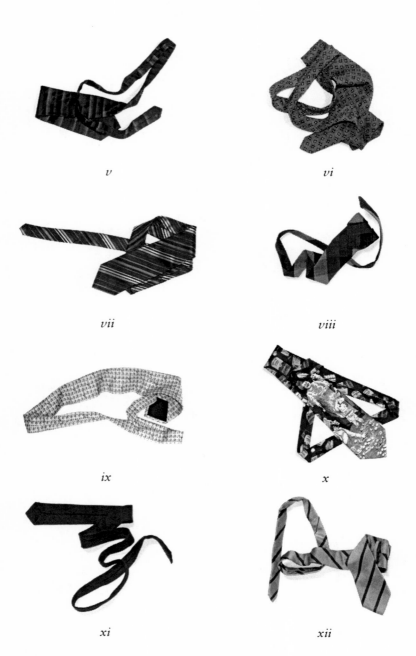

v

vi

vii

viii

ix

x

xi

xii

BOOK XI

5

Blushing a mistake under a carpet of hair.

6

No successes: no successors.

7

Baring all.— The way he undressed suggested he had something to hide.

8

Sin and sincerity have a familial tie; though closer to the spirit of sin is insincerity.

9

Paying homage bankrupts before the payee has time to cash the name cheque.

10

Laughing at your own jokes can sound as stale as re-canned laughter.

11

How many books have you gone to bed with and fallen asleep before the climax?

12

Imagine someone pointing something out to themselves: is this a misunderstanding of the function of pointing?

xiii

xiv

xv

xvi

xvii

xviii

xix

xx

BOOK XI

13

Rubric for a hot head: a lax tongue defames the face.

14

Children carrying churches on their backs.

15

I didn't realise he thought himself so interesting.

16

Heavy hands when it comes to write, but fingers must be light.

17

Haven't you heard? The worm strangled the bird.

18

Gritty like a boiled egg on a nudist beach.

19

An unchanging mind has a blank expression.

20

Tongues burn from lapping up books hot from the press, thinking them to be cool.

21

Trichotillomania: as if you really could pull ideas out of your head.

xxi

xxii

xxiii

xxiv

xxv

xxvi

xxvii

xxviii

22

A puncture is the surest way of bringing you right back down to earth.

23

My whole day was spent saving; whole years may be wasted this way.

24

The marvellous shapes that bodies assume whilst trying to get out of one shape and into another.

25

Pushmi-pullyu.— 'Now' is the path upon which the past and the future ride a two-way-tandem.

26

Why do you read so much? Because I never remember. Why do you never remember? Because I read too much.

27

Celebrity chefs look ugly whilst making something beautiful; normal celebrities look beautiful whilst making something ugly.

28

I overheard a banker casually say over the phone : "All the money he used to spend on guns has now gone because he is being charged thirty grand a year." My first thought was: "Thank God for the financial crisis."

xxix   *xxx*

BOOK XI

29

There is little that does not sour with age, though you, it appears, have soured with youth.

30

Mock fingers stock the mouth with ham.

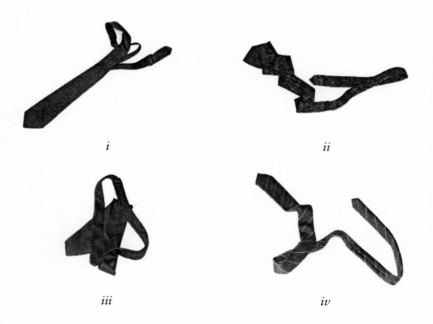

i

ii

iii

iv

BOOK XII

1

Trapped wind speaks for itself.

2

The word prolific sounds to me like vomit: an effortless, uncontrollable movement mars the artist with the itch of creativity; fruitful activity is fine if it springs from the right orifice.

3

Suddenly the failures cement.

4

Could we equally say turning the dark off?

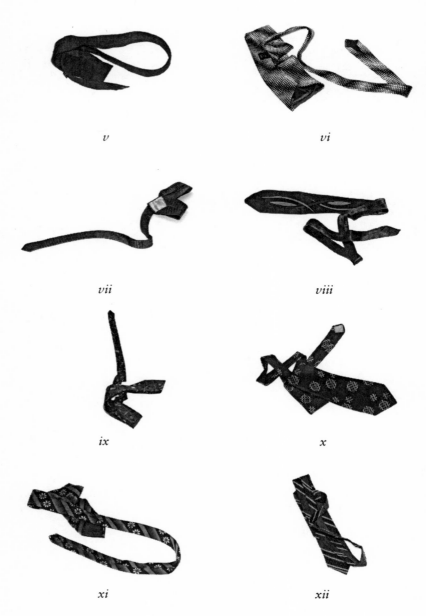

v

vi

vii

viii

ix

x

xi

xii

BOOK XII

5

Memory is a muscle.

6

Sex is an animal-forming habit.

7

You need only know three letters to exist.

8

Good social art is not social, bad social art is not art.

9

Inattention leans open like a door. . . give us our sins and lead us not from our temptation.

10

Open works are shrouded by the drastic shadow of an Either/Aura.

11

At least love your lies enough to practice them to perfection.

12

Loudmouths sentence every passer-by to death.

13

An unfortunate collision of features.

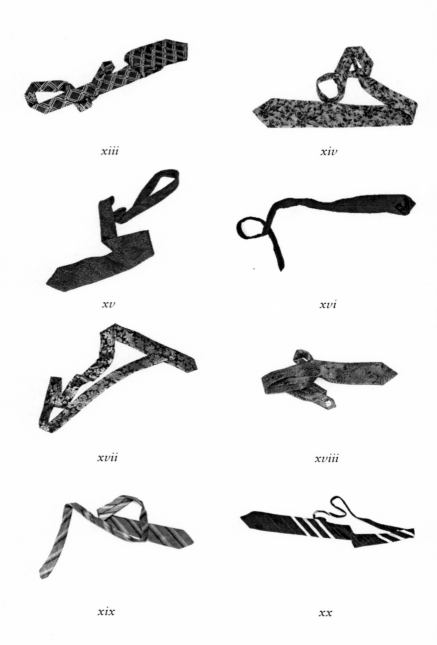

xiii

xiv

xv

xvi

xvii

xviii

xix

xx

BOOK XII

14

Catching money-grubbing words fall from my mouth, I instantly lose my appetite.

15

Polishing truth will reflect more of the polisher.

16

Death-by-radio.

17

I can not count the joys I have hand looking at windows.

18

Unsettling how it settles in a uniform fashion, blank as it is of any information, except that it is dusty. The particular charm of dust lies in its talent for self-organisation. Indiscriminate, epicene, it knows no borders; a true democracy of itinerant lumpen, keeping company amongst the ruins. Dust might sit without waking, softly waiting under a blanket of sleep, to rise again in haste. Swept by the current of form, it hollows a formless assault: detracting from the sheen of things, muddying shine, swarming surface. Dust is the true teller of time, of the minute fall of moments.

19

Life begins in the first act and ends at the first break.

20

How little I have added; but how much I have subtracted.

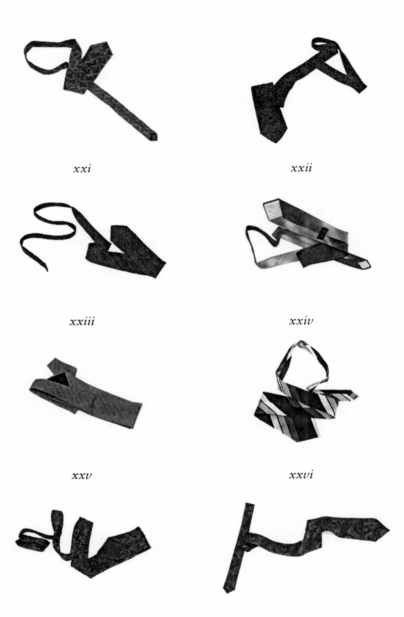

xxi

xxii

xxiii

xxiv

xxv

xxvi

xxvii

xxviii

BOOK XII

21

Telling tales.— Lies help us to balance our lives.

22

Failure consoles intention by giving it another goal.

23

Start with a flat page each day, gradually crumple, fill it with body, wildly dream and slobber, and then discard.

24

In reproduction, the sound of my own laughter mocks me.

25

I misheard you correctly.— Personality is a case of mistaken identity.

26

Life will fill to the brim however hard you try to drink it dry.

27

Take your hands out of my head.

28

New acquaintances have to be worn for a short duration before knowing if they will rub you up the wrong way. The first day may give a favourable impression, but on the second we may find blisters that are sensitive to the touch of a certain phrase, topic of conversation; hardness of soul.

xxix

xxx

xxxi

BOOK XII

29

A rare imagination: occasional thought.

30

The harder you look the tougher it gets.

31

Success is often a paraphrased mistake.

Printed in the United Kingdom by
Lightning Source UK Ltd., Milton Keynes
141494UK00001B/6/P